TH

...TRADITION

Other titles in preparation

PRAYING WITH
The English Tradition

Compiled and introduced by
Margaret Pawley

Foreword by
Robert Runcie

First published 1990
Triangle
SPCK
Holy Trinity Church
Marylebone Road
London NW1 4DU

British Library Cataloguing in Publication Data
Pawley, Margaret
Praying with the English tradition.
1. Christian life. Prayer
I. Title
248.32

ISBN 0-281-04479-1

Typeset by Rowland Phototypesetting Ltd
Bury St Edmunds, Suffolk
Printed in Great Britain by
BPCC Hazell Books Ltd
Aylesbury, Bucks

Contents

Contents

Foreword by
Robert Runcie

What is 'the English tradition'? It is something we find as easy to recognise as our own face in the mirror, yet as hard to describe. Yet, however difficult the description, Margaret Pawley's excellent compilation has caught that elusive quality which many of us would recognise as 'English spirituality'. As we read and use these prayers, we acknowledge and celebrate the fourteen hundred years of English history which informs our own faith. We sense how we take our place within a community, formed in the course of our history, of men and women who have found strength and faith through prayer. The threads we may trace through this collection strengthen our own hold on faith.

One of the strongest features identifying English spirituality was the response made in this country to the tide of reform which swept Europe in the sixteenth century. However, in reading this collection, I was struck by the essential continuity of our tradition. Mediaeval expressions of faith find their place in post-Reformation worship, not only within Anglicanism, but in the prayers of men like Richard Baxter and in those, like John Wesley, whom Anglicanism finally failed to hold. As well as this, the prayers composed in response to special needs speak to us directly across the years in spite of cultural distance. An example is the prayer of Archbishop Benson upon the death of his son. It may be that some of Benson's attitudes now make him seem a strangely remote figure from our own time, but we still recognise and respond to his cry for help in the extremity of grief.

I warmly commend this collection, not only as an aid to prayer, but as a means by which we see ourselves taking our place in a continuing English tradition of faith.

Robert Cantuar

Introduction

A collection such as this can only be partial. It cannot represent the prayers of Englishmen and English-women down the years who have prayed extemporarily, or in silent contemplation, or within the context of the Bible or church services – all within a tradition which is by its nature comprehensive. Loyalty to the *Book of Common Prayer* has encouraged many to use it exclusively and this has hindered the composition of private prayers. For example, Charles Simeon's most recent biographer, Hugh Evan Hopkins, has said that although he has 2000 of Simeon's sermons there are no prayers; for Simeon 'so loved the BCP that he was able to use a Prayer Book collect[1] for almost any situation or occasion'.

There are other difficulties: most of all the tracing of representative prayers. Many fine theologians have left work which will live, but few, if any, prayers; this is true of George Bell and Austin Farrer. I have had an eye to variety of time span, churchmanship, degree of sophistication and subject of petition. Few biographies of religious figures include the prayers they have written. Also, fear of overlapping with other titles in this series, *Praying With the English Poets* and *Praying With the English Mystics*, has limited some of my choices, though I have included a few poets and mystics in the interests of balance; they can be a sample for those who wish to explore further. In common with the rest of the series, I have modernised pronouns in prayers of the last 150 years.

I have restricted my selection to prayers from *English* sources. If I may explain; I have not taken any directly from the earliest Latin liturgical books from the first thousand years AD[2] and all from a source outside England. But I have chosen prayers from the Sarum Missal and Breviary which were revisions of some of these books, carried out at Salisbury from the eleventh century and used extensively in England after that date. I have also felt free to include certain English collects from the *Book of Common Prayer* which were undoubtedly translations from earlier Latin versions from the continent.

Most of the writers of the prayers in this book are, or were, English. There are two exceptions: the first is Anselm. Born in Aosta, now part of Italy, he became to all intents and purposes a Frenchman as a monk of Bec in Normandy, and then one of the greatest Archbishops of Canterbury. The influence in England of his splendid prayers during the centuries following his death, was so considerable that he cannot be excluded. The second name is Joost de Blank; born in Rotterdam, he became an English prelate and champion of racial equality.

Prayers from the Celtic Church in England have been hard to find. Examples which came to hand all happened to derive from Ireland, and not Lindisfarne, and needed to be discarded. This absence of a legacy of writings from the early Northumbrian saints (pre-Bede) is a sad one and leaves a gap. There are some survivals of remarkable prayers from the middle ages whose profound yet straightforward nature gives them enduring value. Some of the best are the prayers of St Edmund Rich, Thomas Bradwardine, the English mystics – chief of whom Julian of Norwich – and, as already mentioned, Anselm.

The medieval *Primers* or *Prymers* which I have used as a source, were prayer books in English designed, during many generations, for the use of the laity of the Church. Though not in any sense 'folk prayers' composed by lay people, they provide remarkable instances of continuity. Several collects in the *Books of Common Prayer*, which date from 1549 onwards, can be traced, though not always perhaps in identical form, in the earlier *Primers*. A case in point is:

> O God, from whom all holy desires, all good counsels and all just works do proceed, give unto us the same peace which the world cannot give . . .

which will, therefore, have been prayed in England, in English, for upwards of seven hundred years. The *Primers* did not include the great central act of devotion, the Eucharist, but rather prayers in the people's own language to be recited at certain times of the day and to meet various circumstances of life. Some examples appear below. At the Reformation, the *Primers* for the laity were revised simultaneously with Matins and Evensong for the *Books of Common Prayer*; the subsequent editions of the *Primer* ran parallel to these Books for the remainder of the sixteenth century.

My chief purpose has been to assemble prayers used down the ages, in which the words and intentions are such that they can be prayed with sincerity and integrity at the end of the twentieth century. When a prayer becomes a part of the pray-er, the Holy Spirit is a part of the praying.

The issues which influenced selection are, then, first the use of language and mode of expression; and secondly, the nature of the petition. Many early English prayers are acceptable today because of a happy choice of words. The particular development of the language with its rich, varied vocabulary, together with an exceptionally gifted body of writers, poets and dramatists in the sixteenth and seventeenth centuries, were crucial in their effect upon religious prose. Moreover, the Latin prayers of an earlier age, with their own beauty of traditional form, accents and rhythms, became translated at this period by men who understood both the ancient style and how it could harmoniously be transposed into English. Two recent translators[3] of Latin collects have commented that the original authors observed certain rules of composition whereby, for instance, clauses and sentences were made to end in definite rhythmic patterns. Because these were understood by the Reformers, this influence can be traced in the English of the *Books of Common Prayer*. For example,

> from whom no secrets are hid

can be more satisfactory than the more strictly grammatical, 'from whom no secrets are hidden'.

For over three hundred years, the distinctive language of the sixteenth and seventeenth centuries, enshrined in the King James version of the Bible, became familiar to English men and women who have read the Scriptures; for Anglicans, this has been true also in respect of the 1662 *Book of Common Prayer*. The language, full of beautiful cadences and associations, has become endowed with a sense of holiness and other-worldliness. For prayers of devotion, many people still find this language a fitting medium through which to speak to God and I have tried to include some examples here.

But many sixteenth-century petitionary prayers, on the other hand, despite their evocative sound, contain elements with which present-day Christians would be less happy. Sickness viewed as divine punishment; requests for the vanquishing of enemies, real or imaginary, which border on paranoia, form the substance of many petitions and hardly reflect the messages of the gospel. Others are uncomfortably self-centred and manipulative; suppliants wallow in sweeping expressions of sinfulness in their pleas for grace:

> Remove from me, O heavenly Father, my lewd, stony, stubborn,
> stinking and unfaithful heart.

and

> Defend us, O Lord, from the terrible plagues of thy
> fearful displeasure.

This type of prayer has not been chosen here.

The prayers of the Caroline Divines, so-called, of the seventeenth century – Lancelot Andrewes, William Laud, John Donne, George Herbert, John Cosin – were free of these excesses. Always aware of their own shortcomings, their gratitude for the loving-kindness of God gives their writings lasting merit. For the same reasons, John Wesley's prayers have a permanent quality. The balance contained in Samuel Johnson's perceptive knowledge of his individual failings and need of grace, commends his prayers to a selection such as this.

Because these are intended to be *usable* prayers, I have not included Nelson's on the morning of Trafalgar. To few is given the responsibility to direct major battles at sea. But I have chosen Laud's prayer on the scaffold with his touching

> Lord, I am coming as fast as I can.

The exact time of our common experience of death is, for most, uncertain but many of us are called to help others at this crucial hour.

During the nineteenth century, the supposed divine satisfaction with the maintenance of the status quo received some knocks. Words of prayer which read:

> This we know, that all things are ordered and sure,
> Everything is ordered with unerring wisdom and
>   unbounded love . . .

were beginning to be questioned, even before the horrors of the First World War, the holocaust and the killing fields of Cambodia. Likewise Mrs Alexander's words:

> The rich man in his castle,
> The poor man at his gate,
> God made them, high or lowly,
> And order'd their estate.

were taken over by what Michael Ramsey has called 'revolutionary claims upon man's social life'.

The merits of the Cross have long been invoked in prayer. Fresh understanding of the meaning of the Incarnation and the implications of the Risen Christ, Emmanuel, God with us, have as a consequence, led to prayer with a changed emphasis. The vision has more love, less fear, greater participation of mankind in God's healing activity in the world:

> May we who share Christ's body live his risen life;
> we who drink his cup bring life to others.

So runs the *Alternative Service Book* of the Church of England. The dynamic, rather than static nature of the English tradition shows itself in more recent prayers to God not wholly Other, far off, but also in all things, all peoples; drawing them into his work for a redeemed creation which Bishop Westcott called '. . . the better order which you have prepared for us'. 'Thy Kingdom come' has taken on a new dimension as mankind recognises the call to share in the process.

> Use us, we pray you, as you will, but always to
> your glory and the welfare of your people

was William Temple's reaction.

> Help us to supply the wants of those who need

is a current grace before meals which accepts the responsibility laid on Christians within the purposes of God.

The English tradition of prayer has given advice not only on what, but also how to pray. The foremost master is the great Anselm with his remarkable assumption:

> . . . I believe so that I may understand, and what is more, I believe that unless I do believe I shall not understand.

Asked by his friends to teach them how to pray, he wrote some prayers for them which he followed by instructions as to what was necessary to prepare the soul to come before God:

> Come now, little man[4]
> turn aside for a while from your daily employment,
> escape for a moment from the tumult of your
>   thoughts.
>   Put aside your weighty cares,
>   let your burdensome distractions wait,
>   free yourself awhile for God
>   and rest awhile in him.
> Enter the inner chamber of your soul,
>   shut out everything except God
>   and that which can help you in seeking him,
>   and when you have shut the door, seek him.
> Now my whole heart, say to God,
>   I seek your face,
> Lord, it is your face I seek.

The second stage is to ask the help of God in this endeavour:

> O Lord my God,
> teach my heart where and how to seek you,
> where and how to find you.

Penitence, recognition of the faithfulness of God, of the power of the Cross, follow, says Anselm, and lead into praise and thanksgiving and towards a vision of glory.

The anonymous author of *The Cloud of Unknowing* (written about 1370) advises a soul at prayer to have '. . . no special thought of anything but God and that thine intent be nakedly directed unto God'. This 'intent', he associates with 'longing' and 'love'. He continues:

Never cease in your intent, but bear ever more on this cloud of unknowing that is between you and your God with a sharp dart of longing love . . .

For, as he declares later, 'short prayer penetrates heaven'.

Evelyn Underhill, speaking to a Fellowship of Prayer, six hundred years later, gave fresh encouragement in the circumstances of the twentieth century:

A real man or woman of prayer should be a live wire, a link between God's grace and the world that needs it . . . agents or transmitters of the transforming, redeeming power of God.

MARGARET PAWLEY

Notes

1   A short form of prayer made up of an invocation, a petition and a pleading of Christ's name or an ascription of glory to God.
2   The Leonine, Gelasian and Gregorian Sacramentaries – liturgical books containing the canon of the Mass and collects.
3   John Willis and Leslie Styler in *Euchologium Anglicanum* (SPCK 1963).
4   Anselm was no chauvinist and wrote several prayers for women.

PRAYERS
FOR ALL TIMES

These our prayers

Let these our prayers, O Lord,
find access to the throne of grace,
through the Son of thy love,
Jesus Christ the righteous;
to whom with thee, O Father,
in the unity of the Spirit,
be all love and obedience,
now and for ever.

John Wesley 1703–91

JOHN WESLEY, preacher and evangelist, was one of the
founders of the Methodist movement, though he remained
a member of the Church of England throughout his life.

For the gifts of the Spirit

Give me, O Lord, I pray thee,
firm faith, unwavering hope,
perfect charity.
Pour into my heart
the spirit of wisdom and understanding,
the spirit of counsel and ghostly strength,
the spirit of knowledge and true godliness,
and the spirit of thy holy fear.
Light eternal, shine in my heart:
Power eternal, deliver me from evil:
Wisdom eternal, scatter the darkness of my
    ignorance:
Might eternal, pity me.
Grant that I may ever seek thy face,
with all my heart and soul and strength;
and, in thine infinite mercy,
bring me at last to thy holy Presence,
where I shall behold thy glory
and possess thy promised joys.

Alcuin 735–804

ALCUIN, theologian and educationalist, was born in York
and educated at the cathedral school. In 781 he met the
Emperor Charlemagne, and became his adviser on matters
of religion and education. Later he was Abbot of Tours.

For a true and living faith

O God, who madest me for thyself,
to show forth thy goodness in me:
Manifest, I humbly beseech thee,
the life-giving power of thy holy nature within me;
help me to such a true and living faith in thee,
such strength of hunger and thirst after
the birth, life and spirit of thy holy Jesus
   in my soul,
that all that is within me,
may be turned from every inward thought
   or outward work
that is not thee, thy holy Jesus,
and heavenly working in my soul.

William Law 1686–1761

WILLIAM LAW is known chiefly for his spiritual writings,
of which the most celebrated was *A Serious Call to a Devout
and Holy Life*.

Lord, thou art in me

Lord, thou art in me
and shalt never be lost out of me,
but I am not near thee
till I have found thee.
Nowhere need I run to seek thee,
but within me where already thou art.
Thou art the treasure hidden within me:
draw me therefore to thee
that I may find thee
and serve and possess thee for ever.

Walter Hilton 13??–1395

WALTER HILTON was one of the English mystics of the
fourteenth century; his *Ladder of Perfection*, on the gift of
contemplation, upon which this extract is based, is his best
known work.

I seek thee

My God, I love thee thyself above all else
and thee I desire as my last end.
Always and in all things,
with my whole heart, and strength
I seek thee.
If thou give not thyself to me,
thou givest nothing;
If I find thee not,
I find nothing.
Grant to me, therefore, most loving God,
that I may ever love thee for thyself
above all things,
and seek thee in all things in this life present,
so that at last I may find thee
and keep thee for ever in the world to come.
   Amen.

Thomas Bradwardine ?1290–1349

THOMAS BRADWARDINE, a native of Chichester and
renowned for his learning, accompanied Edward III on the
continent during his wars with France. Consecrated
Archbishop of Canterbury at Avignon in 1349, he died in the
same year on his return to England, of the Black Death.
Adrian Cruft (d. 1987) wrote an anthem to these words in
1969.

Rescue me

O Lord, rescue me from myself
and give me unto you.
Take away from me all those things
that draw me from you
and give me those things
that lead me to you.

Eric Abbott 1906–83

ERIC ABBOTT, Dean of Westminster from 1959 to 1974,
wrote this prayer for a retreat at Pleshey in September 1959.

I believe so that I may understand

Lord Jesus Christ; Let me seek you by desiring you,
    and let me desire you by seeking you;
    let me find you by loving you,
    and love you in finding you.

    I confess, Lord, with thanksgiving,
    that you have made me in your image,
so that I can remember you, think of you, and love
    you.
But that image is so worn and blotted out by faults,
    and darkened by the smoke of sin,
    that it cannot do that for which it was made,
    unless you renew and refashion it.
Lord, I am not trying to make my way to your
    height,
for my understanding is in no way equal to that,
but I do desire to understand a little of your truth
    which my heart already believes and loves.
I do not seek to understand so that I can believe,
    but I believe so that I may understand;
        and what is more,
I believe that unless I do believe, I shall not
    understand.

Anselm 1033–1109

ANSELM, a native of Aosta, travelled to Normandy and
entered the Abbey of Bec where he later became Abbot. His
friendship with the former Prior, Lanfranc, caused him to
visit England. On Lanfranc's death, Anselm became
Archbishop of Canterbury. The quality of his mind has been
considered outstanding; as also the sweetness of his
character. This prayer was translated from the Latin by
Sister Benedicta Ward SLG.

Keep me ever near to you

Lord keep me ever near to you.
Let nothing separate me from you,
let nothing keep me back from you.
If I fall, bring me back quickly to you,
and make me hope in you,
trust in you,
love you everlastingly.
    Amen.

Edward Bouverie Pusey 1800–82

EDWARD BOUVERIE PUSEY was a leader of the
Tractarians, Regius Professor of Hebrew at Oxford, writer
and preacher.

Make me all yours

Lord, because you have made me,
I owe you the whole of my love;
because you have redeemed me,
I owe you the whole of myself;
because you have promised so much,
I owe you all my being.
Moreover, I owe you
as much more love than myself
    as you are greater than I,
For whom you gave yourself
    and to whom you promised yourself.
I pray you, Lord,
make me taste by love
    what I taste by knowledge;
let me know by love
    what I know by understanding.
I owe you more than my whole self,
but I have no more,
and by myself I cannot render
    the whole of it to you.
Draw me to you, Lord,
in the fullness of love.
I am wholly yours by creation;
make me all yours, too, in love.

Anselm 1033–1109

ANSELM, Abbot of Bec and Archbishop of Canterbury (see
note p. 9). This prayer was translated from the Latin by
Sister Benedicta Ward SLG.

Thou art enough for me

God, of thy goodness,
give me thyself;
for thou art enough for me,
and I may ask nothing
that is less than may be full worship to thee;
and if I ask anything that is less,
I am ever in want:
but only in thee I have all.

Julian of Norwich 1342–?1416

JULIAN, one of the most distinguished of the English
mystics of the fourteenth century, lived as an anchoress in
the city of Norwich. Her *Revelations of Divine Love*, from
which this prayer is taken, record sixteen 'showings' or
revelations which she experienced in 1373.

All my desire thou art

Jesus, receive my heart,
and bring me to thy love.
All my desire thou art.
Kindle fire within me,
that I may win to thy love,
and see thy face in bliss
which shall never cease,
in heaven with never an ending.

Richard Rolle 1295–1349

RICHARD ROLLE was one of the fourteenth-century
English mystics; his writings in Latin and English included
much devotional poetry. He was born and lived for much of
his life in Yorkshire.

Most loving Saviour

Most loving Saviour,
it is written in thy holy gospel,
that thou camest into this world,
not to call the righteous, but sinners,
    to repentance.
Suffer me not, O Lord,
to be of the number of those
    who justify themselves,
who, boasting their own righteousness,
their own works and merits,
despise the righteousness that cometh by faith,
which alone is allowable before thee.
Give me grace to know and acknowledge myself
    as I am,
even the son of wrath by nature;
a wretched sinner, and unprofitable servant,
and wholly to depend on thy merciful goodness
with strong and unshaken faith,
that in this world thou mayest continually call me
unto true repentance, seeing I continually sin,
and in the world to come
bring me unto everlasting glory.

Thomas Becon ?1513–1567

THOMAS BECON, one of the English Reformers, educated
at Cambridge, became chaplain to Archbishop Cranmer. He
fled to the continent during the reign of Queen Mary and
returned to be a Canon of Canterbury during the reign of
Elizabeth I. A prolific writer.

14

Let my feet tread thy paths

When I go into the withdrawing room,
let me consider what my calling is:
let me consider, if a Traitor be hateful,
she that betrays the soul of one is much worse;
the danger, the sin of it.
Then, without pretending to wit,
how quiet and pleasant a thing it is
to be silent, or if I do speak,
that it be to the Glory of God. Lord, assist me.
If they speak of anybody I can't commend,
hold my peace what jest soever they make;

. . .

when they speak filthily,
    tho' I be laughed at, look grave.
Never meddle with others' business,
    nor hardly ask a question;
talk not slightly of religion.
If you speak anything they like,
say 'tis borrowed, and be humble when
    commended.
Before I speak, Lord, assist me;
when I pray, Lord, hear me;
when I am praised, God, humble me;
may the clock, the candle,
    everything I see, instruct me;
Lord, cleanse my hands,
let my feet tread Thy paths.

Margaret Godolphin 1652–78

MARGARET GODOLPHIN was Maid of Honour to the
Queen, (Catherine of Braganza) at the Court of Charles II,
after the Restoration. This prayer was written in 1668 while
Margaret was unmarried and a girl of sixteen.

Our Captain God

O God that art the only hope of the world,
The only refuge for unhappy men,
Abiding in the faithfulness of heaven,
Give me strong succour in this testing place.
O King, protect thy man from utter ruin
Lest the weak faith surrender to the tyrant,
Facing innumerable blows alone.
Remember I am dust, and wind, and shadow,
And life as fleeting as the flower of grass.
But may the eternal mercy which hath shone
From time of old
Rescue thy servant from the jaws of the lion.
Thou who didst come from on high in the cloak of
    flesh,
Strike down the dragon with that two-edged
    sword,
Whereby our mortal flesh can war with the winds
And beat down strongholds, with our Captain
    God.

Bede 675–735

BEDE, Northumbrian monastic scholar and historian is the
source of much of our knowledge of events in Church and
State in his own and earlier times. He was given the title of
Venerable in the ninth century and pronounced a 'Doctor of
the Church' by Pope Leo XIII in 1899. This prayer was
translated by Helen Waddell.

Being a son of God

O Thou who hast redeemed me to be a son of God,
and called me from vanity to inherit all things,
I praise thee that, having loved me
    and given thyself for me,
thou commandest us, saying,
'As I have loved you, so do ye also love
    one another.'
wherein thou hast commanded all men so to love
    me
as to lay down their lives for my peace and
    welfare.
Since love is the end for which
    heaven and earth were made,
enable me to see and discern the sweetness
    of so great a treasure.
And since thou hast advanced me
    into the throne of God,
in the bosom of all angels and men;
commanding them by this precept
to give me a union and communion with thee
    in their dearest affection,
in their highest esteem,
    and in the most near and inward room and seat
    in their hearts;
Give me the grace which St Paul prayed for,
that I may be acceptable to the saints;
Fill me with thy Holy Spirit,
and make my soul and life beautiful;
Make me all wisdom, goodness, and love,
that I may be worthy to be esteemed
    and accepted of them,

That, being delighted also with their felicity,
I may be crowned with thine and with their glory.

Thomas Traherne 1636–74

THOMAS TRAHERNE, a poet of considerable originality
and imagination, was Rector of Credenhill near Hereford.

Day by day

Thanks be to thee, my Lord Jesus Christ,
For all the benefits which thou has given to me,
For all the pains and insults which thou hast
    borne for me.
O most merciful redeemer, friend and brother,
May I know thee more clearly,
Love thee more dearly
And follow thee more nearly,
Day by day.

Richard of Chichester 1197–1253

RICHARD OF CHICHESTER was consecrated Bishop of
Chichester in 1244. He was canonised in 1262. He was
known as a man of deep spirituality and a sound
administrator.

For guidance

Lord God Almighty,
shaper and ruler of all creatures,
I pray thee of thy great mercy,
and for the token of the holy Rood,[1]
Guide me to thy will, to my soul's need,
better than I can myself.
Strengthen me against temptations;
shield me against my foes,
seen and unseen.
Teach me to do Thy will,
that I may inwardly love Thee
    before all things,
with a clean mind and clean body.
For Thou art my Maker and my Redeemer,
My Help, my Comfort, my Trust, my Hope.
Praise and glory be to Thee
now, ever and ever, world without end.

Alfred the Great 849–899

ALFRED 'the Great', King of Wessex from 871, was a
promoter of church reform and the revival of learning.

[1] the Cross

God be in my head

God be in my head,
 and in my understanding;
God be in mine eyes,
 and in my looking;
God be in my mouth,
 and in my speaking;
God be in my heart,
 and in my thinking;
God be at mine end,
 and at my departing.

Anon. medieval

An anonymous prayer of the middle ages, found in *Pynson's Horae*, a book printed in 1514 by Richard Pynson (d. 1530); he was appointed King's Printer on the appointment of Henry VIII and introduced Roman type into England.

King and Lord of all

O Christ, King and Lord of all,
teach me to know that with you
nothing is too bad to be cured;
nothing too good to be hoped for;
nothing too hard to be attempted;
and nothing so precious that it
cannot be surrendered for your sake;
who lives and reigns
with the Father
in the Unity of the Spirit
for ever and ever.

Lesslie Newbigin 1909–

LESSLIE NEWBIGIN, a Northumbrian, was ordained into
the Presbyterian Church of Scotland in 1936, and became a
missionary in India. He was subsequently Bishop in Madura
and Ramnad in the Church of South India, and Bishop in
Madras from 1965 to 1974.

Sweet Saviour Christ

O my sweet Saviour Christ,
which in thine undeserved love towards mankind
so kindly wouldst suffer the painful death
of the Cross,
suffer me not to be cold nor lukewarm
in love again towards thee.

Sir Thomas More 1478–1535

SIR THOMAS MORE was appointed Lord Chancellor of
England in 1529. In 1535 he was executed on the grounds of
high treason for his opposition to the Act of Supremacy of
Henry VIII.

Blessed Jesu

O Blessed Jesu,
my Lord and my God,
who has opened the kingdom of heaven
to all believers,
help me not to close,
through my own fault,
that door against myself.

Edward King 1829–1910

EDWARD KING, Bishop of Lincoln, is remembered for his holiness of life and care for individuals. This prayer is taken from his *Meditations on the Seven Words from the Cross* of 1874.

Every heart stands open

To you, O God,
every heart stands open
and every will speaks;
no secret is hidden from you.
I implore you
so to purify the intention of my heart
with the gift of your grace
that I may love you perfectly
and praise you worthily.
Amen.

Anon. *c.* 1370

This prayer comes from *The Cloud of Unknowing*, a book of
devotion by an anonymous writer of the fourteenth century.

O Lord, my God

Cause me, O Lord my God,
More and more to comprehend and acknowledge
   What I owe you,
   What I owe others,
   What I owe myself.

Eric Milner-White 1884–1963

ERIC MILNER-WHITE, Dean of York from 1941–1963, was a
noted composer and compiler of books of prayers. This
prayer is taken from *My God, My Glory*.

His words to Christ, going to the Cross

When Thou wast taken, Lord, I oft have read,
All Thy disciples Thee forsook, and fled.
Let their example not a pattern be
For me to fly but now to follow Thee.

Robert Herrick 1591–1674

ROBERT HERRICK, clergyman and poet, was the
incumbent of a parish in Devon from which he was evicted
during the Commonwealth; he was reinstated in 1662.
Much of his poetry reflected the countryside where he lived;
this poem is entitled 'His words to Christ, going to the
Cross'.

Blessing

Jesus Christ, you child so wise,
Bless my hands and fill my eyes.
And bring my soul to Paradise.

Hilaire Belloc 1870–1953

HILAIRE BELLOC was of French origin, but his family
settled in England where he became a prolific and versatile
writer.

Waiting and longing for our Lord

Keep me, O Lord, while I tarry on this earth,
   in a daily serious seeking after thee,
    and in a believing affectionate walking with
      thee.
That,
when thou comest, we may be found
   not hiding our talent,
   nor serving our flesh,
   nor yet asleep with our lamp unfurnished;
But waiting and longing for our Lord,
   our glorious God for ever and ever.   Amen.

Richard Baxter 1615–91

RICHARD BAXTER, the Puritan divine, was a prolific writer
and champion of moderation.

Living in perfect charity

Grant, O God, that we may keep a constant guard
upon our thoughts and passions,
that they may never lead us into sin;
that we may live in perfect charity with all
     mankind,
in affection to those that love us,
and in forgiveness to those,
if any there are, that hate us.
Give us good and virtuous friends.
In the name of our blessed Lord
     and Saviour Jesus Christ.

Warren Hastings 1732–1818

WARREN HASTINGS, English statesman, was
Governor-General of Bengal from 1773 to 1784.

Commiting ourselves to thee

Cleanse our minds, O Lord we beseech thee,
of all anxious thoughts for ourselves,
that we may learn not to trust
in the abundance of what we have,
save as tokens of thy goodness and grace,
but that we may commit ourselves in faith
   to thy keeping,
and devote all our energy of soul, mind and body
To the work of thy kingdom
And the furthering of the purposes
   of thy divine righteousness;
Through Jesus Christ our Lord.

Euchologium Anglicanum

Euchologium Anglicanum, translations from the Latin of early sacramentaries used in England during the middle ages, edited by John Willis and Leslie Styler.

In your will is our peace

Almighty Father,
in whose hands are our lives:
we commend ourselves to the keeping of your
    love.
In your will is our peace.
In life or in death,
in this world and the next,
uphold us that we may put our trust in you;
through Jesus Christ our Lord.

William Temple 1881–1944

WILLIAM TEMPLE was successively Bishop of Manchester,
Archbishop of York and Archbishop of Canterbury. He was
prominent in national and international fields in the
interests of social and economic justice and Christian unity.

Evening Prayer

O God, from whom all holy desires,
all good counsels,
and all just works do proceed;
Give unto us the same peace
which the world cannot give;
that our hearts being obedient to thy
    commandments,
and the fear of our enemies taken away,
our time may be peaceable through thy protection.
by Christ our Lord.

The *Prymer* of 1539

The *Prymer* of 1539 was named 'The Manual of Prayers or the
Prymer in English'; the second of the reign of Henry VIII.
This prayer occurs in a slightly different form in the 1662
Book of Common Prayer as a Collect at Evening Prayer.

Saviour of the world

Jesus, saviour of the world,
come to us in your mercy:
   we look to you to save and help us.

By your cross and your life laid down
you set your people free:
   we look to you to save and help us.

When they were ready to perish
you saved your disciples:
   we look to you to come to our help.

In the greatness of your mercy
loose us from our chains:
   forgive the sins of all your people.

Make yourself known as our saviour
and mighty deliverer:
   save and help us that we may praise you.

Come now and dwell with us, Lord Christ Jesus:
   hear our prayer and be with us always.

And when you come in your glory:
   make us to be one with you
   and to share the life of your kingdom.

The Alternative Service Book 1980

From the office of Morning Prayer

34

That we may love thee with our whole strength

O God, who through the grace of thy Holy Spirit,
dost pour the gift of love
   into the hearts of thy faithful people:
Grant unto us health, both of mind and body,
that we may love thee with our whole strength,
and with entire satisfaction
may perform those things
Which are pleasing unto thee,
Through Christ our Lord.

The Sarum Breviary

During the middle ages, the Roman rite was modified for
use at the cathedral of Salisbury, and spread throughout
England, known as the Sarum rite. The Sarum books were
used by the Reformers in the compilation of the *Books of
Common Prayer*.

For wholeness

O Lord, penetrate those murky corners
where we hide memories and tendencies
on which we do not care to look,
but which we will not disinter
    and yield freely up to you,
that you may purify and transmute them.
The persistent buried grudge,
the half-acknowledged enmity
which is still smouldering;
the bitterness of that loss
    we have not turned into sacrifice,
the private comfort we cling to,
the secret fear of failure which saps our initiative
and is really inverted pride;
the pessimism which is an insult to your joy, Lord,
we bring all these to you,
and we review them with shame and penitence
in your steadfast light.

Evelyn Underhill 1875–1941

EVELYN UNDERHILL is remembered particularly for her
writings on mysticism and as a spiritual counsellor.

For love in action

O Lord, we most humbly beseech thee to give us
   grace
not only to be hearers of the Word,
but also doers of the same;
not only to love,
but also to live thy gospel;
not only to profess,
but also to practise thy blessed commandments,
unto the honour of thy holy name.

Thomas Becon ?1513–1567

THOMAS BECON, English Reformer (see note on p. 14).

Dwelling in love

O God, we have known and believed
the love that you have for us.
May we, by dwelling in love,
   dwell in you,
   and you in us.
Teach us, O heavenly Father,
the love wherewith you have loved us;
fashion us, O blessed Lord,
after your own example of love;
shed abroad, O you Holy Spirit of love,
the love of God and man in our hearts.
For your name's sake.

Henry Alford 1810–71

HENRY ALFORD, Dean of Canterbury from 1857 to 1871,
was a scholar and writer of hymns and poetry.

Suffer us not to undervalue ourselves

Eternal and most glorious God,
who hast stamped the soul of man with thine
    Image,
received it into thy Revenue,
and made it a part of thy Treasure;
Suffer us not so to undervalue ourselves,
nay, so to impoverish thee
as to give away these souls for nothing,
and all the world is nothing
if the soul must be given for it.
Do this, O God,
for his sake who knows our natural infirmities,
for he had them,
and knows the weight of our sins,
for he paid a dear price for them,
thy Son, our Saviour Jesus Christ.   Amen.

John Donne 1573–1631

JOHN DONNE, poet, and Dean of St Paul's from 1621 to
1631.

Knowing you are there

Lord, give us grace to hold to you
   when all is weariness and fear
   and sin abounds within, without
   when love itself is tested by the doubt . . .
   that love is false, or dead within the soul,
   when every act brings new confusion, new
   distress,
   new opportunities, new misunderstandings,
   and every thought new accusation.

Lord, give us grace that we may know
   that in the darkness pressing round
   it is the mist of sin that hides your face,
   that you are there
   and you do know we love you still
   and our dependence and endurance in your will
   is still our gift of love.

Gilbert Shaw 1886–1967

GILBERT SHAW was a notable writer, retreat conductor
and spiritual counsellor.

Thanksgiving

At thy hands, O Lord our God,
we beg thy gracious acceptance
of our humble praise and thanksgiving,
for all thy blessings, spiritual and temporal,
so freely conferred upon us.
We praise thee for all the comforts
   and conveniences of this life,
and for all the means and hopes of a better:
particularly for what we have received this day;
the food of our souls set before us,
the Word of salvation sounding in our ears,
and the Spirit of God striving in our hearts.
Oh, withdraw not thy tender mercies from us,
but still continue thy accustomed goodness,
and increase thy grace and heavenly blessings
   upon us,
And rejoice over us to do us good.

John Wesley 1703–91

JOHN WESLEY was one of the founders of Methodism (see
note on p. 3). This prayer comes from *A Collection of
Prayers for Families* published by him in 1779.

Light invisible

O Light Invisible, we praise Thee!
Too bright for mortal vision.
O Greater Light, we praise Thee for the less;
The eastern light our spires touch at morning,
The light that slants upon our western doors at
    evening,
The twilight over stagnant pools at batflight,
Moon light and star light, owl and moth light,
Glow-worm glowlight on a grassblade.
O Light Invisible, we worship Thee!

  We thank Thee for the lights that we have
     kindled,
The light of altar and of sanctuary;
Small lights of those who meditate at midnight
And lights directed through the coloured panes of
    windows
And light reflected from the polished stone,
The gilded carven wood, the coloured fresco.
Our gaze is submarine, our eyes look upward
And see the light that fractures through unquiet
    water.
We see the light but see not whence it comes.
O Light Invisible, we glorify Thee!

T. S. Eliot 1888–1965

From Chorus X, Choruses from 'The Rock'.

42

Love was his meaning

I learned that love was our Lord's meaning.
And I saw for certain, both here and elsewhere,
that before ever he made us, God loved us;
and that his love has never slackened,
   nor ever shall.
In this love all his works have been done,
and in this love he has made everything serve us;
and in this love our life is everlasting.
Our beginning was when we were made,
but the love in which he made us
   never had beginning.
In it we have our beginning.
All this we shall see in God for ever.
May Jesus grant this.   Amen.

Julian of Norwich 1342–1416

JULIAN, anchoress and mystic (see note on p. 12).

For charity

O Lord, who hast taught us
that all our doings without charity are nothing
     worth;
Send thy Holy Spirit and pour into our hearts
that excellent gift of charity,
the very bond of peace and of all virtues,
without which whosoever liveth
is counted dead before thee;
Grant this for thine only Son
Jesus Christ's sake.   Amen.

The First Prayer Book of Edward VI, 1549

This prayer is attributed to Thomas Cranmer 1489–1556,
Archbishop of Canterbury from 1532. It also occurs in the
1662 *Book of Common Prayer*, as the Collect for the Sunday
next before Lent, and in a modernised form in the *Alternative
Service Book 1980* as the Collect for the Seventh Sunday after
Pentecost.

Come, Holy Spirit

Come thou Holy Spirit	Veni, Sancte Spiritus
Send from highest heaven	Et emitte coelitus
Radiance of thy light.	Lucis tuae radium.
Come, father of the poor	Veni, pater pauperum,
Come, giver of all gifts	Veni, dator munerum,
Come, light of every heart.	Veni, lumen cordium.
Of comforters the best	Consolator optime,
Dear guest of every soul	Dulcis hospes animae,
Refreshment ever sweet.	Dulce refrigerium.
In our labour rest	In labore requies,
Coolness in our heat	In aestu temperies,
Comfort in our grief.	In fletu solatium.
O most blessed light	O lux beatissima,
Fill the inmost hearts	Remple cordis intima
Of thy faithful ones.	Tuorum fidelium.
Without thy holy presence	Sine tuo numine,
All is dark	Nihil est in lumine,
Nothing free from sin.	Nihil est innoxium.
What is soiled cleanse	Lava quod est sordidum,
What is dry refresh	Riga quod est aridum,
What is wounded heal.	Sana quod est saucium.
What is rigid bend	Flecte quod est rigidum,
What is frozen warm	Fove quod est frigidum,
Guide what goes astray.	Rege quod est devium.

Give thy faithful ones	Da tuis fidelibus,
Who in thee confide	In te confidentibus,
Sevenfold hallowing.	Sacrum septenarium.
Give goodness its reward	Da virtutis meritum,
Give journey safe through	
death	Da salutis exitum,
Give joy that has no end.	Da perenne gaudium.

Anon, 13th century translated by George Appleton
1902–

This thirteenth-century prayer for the feast of Pentecost has
often been attributed to Archbishop Stephen Langton.

PRAYERS
FOR SPECIAL TIMES

Advent

Almighty God, give us grace
that we may cast away the works of darkness,
and put upon us the armour of light,
now in the time of this mortal life,
in which thy Son Jesus Christ
came to visit us in great humility;
that in the last day,
when he shall come again in his glorious Majesty
to judge both the quick and the dead,
we may rise to the life immortal,
Through him who liveth and reigneth
with thee and the Holy Ghost,
Now and ever.   Amen.

The First Prayer Book of Edward VI, 1549

This prayer also appears as the Collect for the First Sunday
in Advent in the 1662 *Book of Common Prayer*, and in a
modernised form in the *Alternative Service Book 1980*.

The Passion

Lord, what is man? why should he cost thee
   So dear? what had his ruin lost thee?
Lord what is man, that thou hast over-bought
   So much a thing of nought?

. . .

O my Saviour, make me see,
How dearly thou hast paid for me,
That Lost again my life may prove,
As then in Death, so now in Love.

Richard Crashaw 1612–49

RICHARD CRASHAW, the son of a Puritan divine, went
into exile during the Civil War and died in Italy as a Roman
Catholic. Much of his poetry was filled with a strong
religious feeling. This prayer is taken from *Caritas Nimia*, or
The Dear Bargain, from *Steps to the Temple*, 1648.

The Passion

Now, our Lord Jesus Christ,
give us grace, so to honour God,
and to love our fellow Christians,
and ourselves to be lowly of heart,
that we may for our honouring be honoured,
for our love be loved,
and for our meekness be lifted up
into the high bliss of heaven,
that Jesus bought for us
with his blood and most precious Passion.
So be it.   Amen.

Edmund Rich 1170–1240

EDMUND RICH became Archbishop of Canterbury in 1233.
He was canonised in 1247. This prayer is adapted and
translated from the Latin of his *Speculum Ecclesiae*.

Easter

Lord Jesus, risen from the dead
   and alive for evermore;
stand in our midst tonight
   as in the upper room;
show us your hands and your side;
speak your peace to our hearts and minds;
and send us forth into the world
   as your witnesses;
for the glory of your name.

John R. W. Stott 1921–

JOHN R. W. STOTT is Rector Emeritus of All Souls,
Langham Place, London, where he was rector from 1950 to
1975. He is a leading Evangelical preacher and writer.

52

For the beginning of a new year

O Eternal Lord Christ,
who are the First and the Last, and the Living One,
and who in your mercy has brought us safely
to the beginning of another year:
Accept our thanksgiving for the blessings of the
    past,
renew our strength and courage in the present,
and direct all our way into the future;
for your honour and glory,
who are the same yesterday, today and for ever.

Frank Colquhoun 1909–

FRANK COLQUHOUN was a Canon Residentiary of
Southwark and later Vice-Dean of Norwich; he is a
considerable writer and collector of prayers.

53

Holy Communion

What was it that Paul received of the Lord?
God, of his mercy open our hearts:
to see our errors, and content ourselves
    to be ordered by the wisdom of God,
to do that God will have us to do,
to believe that God will have us to believe,
to worship that God will have us worship.
So shall we have comfort of the holy mysteries;
so shall we receive the fruits of Christ's death;
so shall we be partakers of Christ's body and
    blood;
so shall Christ truly dwell in us,
and we in him.
So shall all error be taken from us;
so shall we join all together in God's truth;
so shall we all be able,
    with one heart and one spirit,
to know and to glorify
the only, the true, and the living God,
and his only-begotten Son Jesus Christ;
to whom both with the Holy Ghost
    be all honour and glory
For ever and ever.   Amen.

John Jewel 1522–71

JOHN JEWEL was a leading Reformer, famed for his
intellect, who went into exile in Germany in 1555 and
returned in the reign of Elizabeth I. He became Bishop of
Salisbury in 1560. This extract comes from a sermon
delivered at St Paul's Cross in that year.

At Holy Communion

Glory be to thee, O Jesus, my Lord and my God,
for thus feeding my soul
with thy most blessed Body and Blood.
Oh, let thy heavenly food
   transfuse new life and new vigour
   into my soul,
and into the souls of all that communicate with
   me,
that our faith may daily increase;
that we may all grow more humble and contrite
   for our sins;
that we may all love thee and serve thee,
and delight in thee,
and praise thee
more fervently, more incessantly,
than ever we have done heretofore.

Thomas Ken 1637–1711

THOMAS KEN was Bishop of Bath and Wells in the late
seventeenth century. Having taken an oath of allegiance to
James II before the king went into exile, he refused to take
the oath to William III. Deposed from his see, he lived in
retirement as one of the Non-jurors. He wrote a number of
hymns and prayers.

At Holy Communion

Glory to thee, Almighty Father,
who hast provided for them that love thee
the Bread of life,
that we may be ever mindful of thy wonderful
    mercy
in sending to us thine only begotten Son,
born of the Virgin Mary.
Glory to thee, O Heavenly Father,
for when we were not,
thou didst give unto us existence,
and when we were sinners
thou didst grant unto us a Saviour.
Glory to thee, through the same,
thy Son our Lord and God,
Who with thee and the Holy Ghost
doth govern all things, world without end.

Dunstan *c.* 909–88

DUNSTAN, Archbishop of Canterbury from 959 to 988, was
a restorer of the monastic life and supporter of the cause of
learning in England. He preached for the last time on
Ascension Day 988, when these words were recorded.

56

After Communion

Father of all, we give you thanks and praise,
that when we were still far off
you met us in your Son and brought us home.
Dying and living, he declared your love,
gave us grace,
and opened the gate of glory.
May we who share Christ's body
live his risen life;
we who drink his cup
bring life to others;
we whom the Spirit lights
give life to the world.
Keep us firm
in the hope you have set before us,
so we and all your children shall be free,
and the whole earth live to praise your name;
through Christ our Lord.   Amen.

The Alternative Service Book, 1980

The Bible, the Word

And I pray thee, merciful Jesus,
that as Thou has graciously granted me
to drink down sweetly from the Word
    which tells of Thee,
so wilt Thou kindly grant
that I may come at length to Thee,
the fount of all wisdom,
and stand before Thy face for ever.

Bede 675–735

BEDE, Northumbrian monk and historian (see note on p. 16). With this prayer he ended his *Ecclesiastical History of the English People* in 731.

For an understanding of the Bible

Blessed Lord, who hast caused all holy Scriptures
to be written for our learning;
Grant that we may in such wise hear them,
read, mark, learn and inwardly digest them,
that by patience, and comfort of thy holy Word,
we may embrace, and ever hold fast
the blessed hope of everlasting life,
which thou hast given us
in our Saviour Jesus Christ.   Amen.

First Prayer Book of Edward VI 1549

This prayer also occurs as the Collect for the Third Sunday
in Advent in the 1662 *Book of Common Prayer*, and in a
modern form in the *Alternative Service Book 1980*.

'While reading St John's Gospel'

Lord Jesus, as I read the Gospel of your disciple,
show me what I shall hear and receive and do.
Make this Gospel a living word to me.
Come, Holy Spirit,
help me as I read the Gospel story,
to know the presence of Jesus.
Come, Holy Spirit, warm my heart,
stir my imagination,
open my eyes,
that I may see Jesus and hear his words
and be ready to do what he wills.

Arthur Michael Ramsey 1904–88

ARTHUR MICHAEL RAMSEY was Regius Professor of
Divinity at Cambridge 1950–52, Archbishop of York 1956–61
and Archbishop of Canterbury 1961–74. This prayer is taken
from his book, *Lent with St John*, 1980.

For our country

Let your mercy and blessing, O Lord of lords,
rest upon our land and nation;
upon all the powers which you have ordained over
    us:
Our Queen and those in authority under her,
the ministers of state,
and the great councils of the nation;
that we may lead a quiet and peaceable life
    in all godliness and honesty.
Rule the hearts of our people
    in your faith and fear;
rebuke the power of unbelief and superstition;
and preserve to us your pure Word
    in its liberty and glory
even to the end of days;
through Jesus Christ our Lord.

Handley C. G. Moule 1841–1921

HANDLEY C. G. MOULE, bishop, theologian and writer,
was a leading Evangelical in the Church of England. He was
the first principal of Ridley Hall, Cambridge, and became
Bishop of Durham in 1901.

For leaders

We lift up our hearts, O Lord,
in intercession for all who carry
   civic and political responsibilities.
Grant that, putting aside all merely
   selfish ambition,
they may seek to be the instruments of your will
and carry out your purpose
   for the welfare of your people;
and may they both seek and see your glory
in happier human lives;
through Jesus Christ our Lord.

Leslie D. Weatherhead 1893–1976

LESLIE D. WEATHERHEAD, preacher, writer and healer,
was for many years minister of the City Temple, London,
and President of the Methodist Conference 1955–6.

For the ordering of society

Behold, O Lord God,
our strivings after a truer and more abiding order.
Give us visions that bring back a lost glory
   to the earth,
and dreams that foreshadow the better order
   which you have prepared for us.

Scatter every excuse of frailty and unworthiness:
consecrate us all with a heavenly mission:
open to us a clearer prospect of our work.
Give us strength according to our day
gladly to welcome and gratefully to fulfil it;
through Jesus Christ our Lord.

Brooke Foss Westcott 1825–1901

BROOKE FOSS WESTCOTT was Regius Professor of
Divinity at Cambridge from 1870, and later Bishop of
Durham, from 1890. Westcott House for the training of
clergy and the Cambridge Mission to Delhi owe much to his
initiative; he was also much concerned with social problems.

In times of strife

O God, who are the Father of all,
and who alone makes men to be of one mind:
We ask you, at this time of strife and unrest,
to grant to us
   by the inspiration of your Holy Spirit
a fuller realisation of our brotherhood,
   man with man.
Allay all anger and bitterness,
and deepen in us a sense of truth and equity
in our dealings one with another,
for the sake of your Son, our Lord Jesus Christ.

Randall T. Davidson 1848–1930

RANDALL T. DAVIDSON was successively Bishop of
Rochester and of Winchester, before he became Archbishop
of Canterbury in 1903. Until his resignation in 1928 he was
required to lead the Church of England through years of
considerable change and difficulty. They included the Great
War and the General Strike.

In times of national anxiety

Almighty God,
who has ordained that men should serve you
by serving one another by their labours:
Have regard, we pray you, to this nation,
oppressed at this time by many burdens.
Grant to its citizens grace to work together
with honest and faithful hearts,
each caring for the good of all;
That seeking first your kingdom
    and its righteousness,
they may have added to them all things needful
for their daily wants and the common good;
through Jesus Christ our Lord.

Geoffrey Fisher 1887–1972

GEOFFREY FISHER was Archbishop of Canterbury from
1945 to 1961.

For social and economic justice

O God, the King of righteousness,
lead us, we pray you,
in the ways of justice and of peace;
Inspire us to break down
    all tyranny and oppression,
to gain for every man his due reward
and from every man his due service;
that each may live for all,
and all may care for each,
in the name of Jesus Christ.

William Temple 1881–1944

WILLIAM TEMPLE was Archbishop of Canterbury from
1942 to 1944 (see note on p. 32).

For the oppressed

Strengthen us, O God,
to relieve the oppressed,
to hear the groans of poor prisoners,
to reform the abuses of all professions;
that many be made not poor
to make a few rich;
for Jesus Christ's sake.

Oliver Cromwell 1599–1658

OLIVER CROMWELL, Lord Protector of England during
the Commonwealth. This prayer is adapted from a letter
which he wrote after the Battle of Dunbar 1650.

For the hungry

O merciful and living Father,
look in your mercy, we pray you,
on the many millions who are hungry in the world
and at the mercy of disease.
Grant that we who have lived so comfortably
and gently all our lives
may have true sympathy with them
and do all in our power,
as individuals and as a nation,
to help them to that abundant life
which is your will for them;
through Jesus Christ our Lord.   Amen.

George Appleton 1902–

GEORGE APPLETON, a distinguished modern writer and
compiler of prayers, was Archbishop of Perth from 1963 to
1969, and Archbishop in Jerusalem from 1969 to 1974.

For those in poverty

O God, our heavenly Father,
have mercy upon all who are in poverty
    and distress.
Be their succour and defence,
provide them with food and clothing
    sufficient for their bodily needs,
and grant them day by day
    to cast all their care upon you.
Help us in some way to help them;
through Jesus Christ our Lord.

John Hunter 1849–1917

JOHN HUNTER was minister of the Independent chapel
King's Weigh House in London.

For those in need

To thy faithfulness and protection,
O dearest Father,
I commit all that concerneth me,
especially wife, children, friends
and such as thou hast put under my governance.
Comfort and help thou
all those that lie in bonds,
and are persecuted for thy Word's sake.
Have mercy upon all such as are in prison,
poverty, sickness and heaviness.
Oh bring thou the whole world
to the knowledge of thy holy word,
that they may live according to thy godly will,
and throughout all troubles
to endure and continue still
in the Christian faith.

Miles Coverdale 1488–1568

MILES COVERDALE, Reformer, while in exile on the
Continent translated the complete Bible into English. He
returned to England to become Bishop of Exeter in 1551.

For racial unity

O God, who has called us
  into the fellowship of your dear Son;
Draw into closer unity, we ask you,
the people of all races in this and every land;
that in fellowship with you
they may understand and help one another,
and that, serving you,
  they may find their perfect freedom;
through the same your Son Jesus Christ our Lord.

Joost de Blank 1908–68

JOOST DE BLANK became Bishop of Stepney in 1952 and
was Archbishop of Cape Town from 1957 to 1963. He was a
life-long worker for good relations between the races of the
world.

Reverence for life

Eternal Father,
source of life and light,
whose love extends to all people,
all creatures, all things;
Grant us that reverence for life
which becomes those who believe in you;
lest we despise it, degrade it,
or come callously to destroy it.
Rather let us save it,
secure it, and sanctify it,
after the example of your Son,
Jesus Christ our Lord.

Robert Runcie 1921–

ROBERT RUNCIE, Archbishop of Canterbury 1980–1991.

For the unity of Christendom

O God, who of thy great goodness
   has united us into thy holy Church
   the mystical body of thy Son:
We, as living members thereof,
mourning with them that mourn
and rejoicing with them that do rejoice,
present our supplications and prayers
at the throne of thy grace
on behalf of all the Churches;
beseeching thee to look down
   in an especial manner,
   with an eye of mercy and pity,
upon the sad and mournful estate
   of such of them as still labour
   under any troubles or persecutions
   for righteousness' sake.
Suffer not thine enemies to triumph
   over thine heritage.
Plead thy cause with them
   who corrupt thy truth
   and afflict thy servants.
Show thyself to be their mighty deliverer,
that all men may see it, and say,
'Verily there is a God that judgeth in the earth.'
Enlighten those who are in darkness and error,
and open their eyes to the acknowledgement
   of thy truth;

that so we may all become one flock
under one great Shepherd
and Bishop of our souls,
Jesus Christ our Lord.

William Wake 1657–1737

WILLIAM WAKE, Archbishop of Canterbury from 1716,
had a particular concern for good relations with the Roman
Catholic and Reformed Churches of Europe; he carried on a
prolonged correspondence with theologians at the
Sorbonne in Paris, with a view to a plan of reunion.

For those newly married

O Blessed Father,
never suffer any mistakes or discontent,
any distrustfulness or sorrow,
any trifling arrests of fancy
    or unhandsome accident,
to cause any unkindness betwixt us:
but let us so dearly love,
so affectionately observe,
so religiously attend to each other's
    good and content,
that we may always please thee,
and by this learn and practise
    our duty and greatest love to thee,
and become mutual helps to each other
in the way of godliness;
that when we have received the blessings
    of a married life –
The comforts of society,
the endearments of a holy and great affection,
and the dowry of blessed children –
we may for ever dwell together
in the embraces of thy love and glories,
feasting in the Marriage Supper of the Lamb
to eternal ages,
through Jesus Christ our Lord.

Jeremy Taylor 1613–67

JEREMY TAYLOR was bishop successively of various Irish
sees; a scholar and writer of devotional works, including
many prayers.

On the birth of a child

O Lord God,
in whose hands are the issues of life,
we thank you for the life given
and the life preserved.
And as you have knit together
   life and love in one fellowship,
so we pray you to grant
that with this fresh gift of life to us,
there may be given an increase of love
   one to another.
Grant that the presence of weakness
   may awaken our tenderness;
enable us to minister to him/her
   who has been given to us
In all lovingness, wisdom and fidelity;
And grant that he/she may live as your child,
And may serve this generation
   according to your will;
Through Jesus Christ our Lord.

William Boyd Carpenter 1841–1918

WILLIAM BOYD CARPENTER was consecrated Bishop of
Ripon in 1884. He founded the Ripon Clergy College which
became Ripon Hall, Oxford, and was honoured in his time
for his preaching.

At a baptism

Look down from heaven, O Lord,
upon thy flock and lambs;
bless their bodies and their souls;
And grant that they
who have received thy sign, O Christ,
on their foreheads
may be thine own in the day of judgement;
through Jesus Christ our Lord.   Amen.

Egbert ?–766

EGBERT, brother to the King of Northumbria, became
Archbishop of York in 732. A noted theologian and teacher,
he also founded the cathedral school.

The evening of life

The day is gone,
and I give thee thanks, O Lord,
   Evening is at hand,
   make it bright unto us.
   As day has its evening
   so also has life;
   the even of life is age;
   age has overtaken me,
   make it bright unto us.
Cast me not away in the time of age;
   forsake me not when my strength faileth me.

Even to my old age be thou He,
and even to hoar hairs carry me;
   do thou make, do thou bear,
   do thou carry and deliver me.
   Abide with me, Lord,
   for it is toward evening,
   and the day is far spent
   of this fretful life.
Let thy strength be made perfect
   in my weakness.

Lancelot Andrewes 1555–1626

LANCELOT ANDREWES was successively Bishop of
Chichester, Ely and Winchester. His book of private
devotions, *Preces Privatae*, was first published in 1648 and
has been used through the following centuries. This poem,
written in Greek, was translated by John Henry Newman.

Our work

O Lord, give your blessing, we pray you, to our
    work.
all our powers of body and mind are yours,
and we would fain devote them to your service.
So bless our efforts,
that they may bring forth in us
The fruits of true wisdom;
through Jesus Christ our Lord.

Thomas Arnold 1795–1842

THOMAS ARNOLD was Headmaster of Rugby School from
1828 to 1841. He wrote this prayer for use by the school.

Good works

God give us grace as we go hence,
Such works to work while we be here.
That after our death Do-well may say,
At the day of doom, we did as he taught.

William Langland ?1330–?1400

WILLIAM LANGLAND, fourteenth-century poet, is
generally considered to be the author of *The Vision
Concerning Piers Plowman*, from which this extract is taken.

Evening hymn

Sun of my soul! Thou Saviour dear,
It is not night if Thou be near:
Oh! may no earth-born cloud arise
To hide Thee from Thy servant's eyes.

. . .

Abide with me from morn till eve,
For without Thee I cannot live:
Abide with me when night is nigh,
For without Thee I dare not die.

John Keble 1792–1866

JOHN KEBLE was a leader of the Tractarian movement,
poet and author of *The Christian Year*, from which this poem,
'Evening', is taken.

Evening Prayer

I lay me down to rest,
in the name of the Father, of the Son
   and of the Holy Ghost.
I thank thee, my heavenly Father,
by thy dear beloved Son Jesus Christ,
that this day of thy plenteous rich mercy
thou has thus preserved me.
I pray thee, forgive me all my sins
which I have this day unrighteously committed
in deed, in word and in thought.
And that thou wouldst vouchsafe
   of thy gracious goodness,
to keep me this night;
for I commit myself
both body and soul and all mine,
Into thy hands. Amen.

The Prymer of 1539

The *Prymer* of 1539 was named 'The Manual of Prayers
or the Prymer in English'; the second of the reign of
Henry VIII.

For nightly protection

Lighten our darkness, we beseech thee, O Lord;
and by that great mercy defend us
from all perils and dangers of this night;
for the love of thine only Son
our Saviour Jesus Christ.

The *Primer*, temp. Elizabeth I

This prayer appeared in 'The Primer set forth at large for the use of the faithful', as revised and issued in the reign of Queen Elizabeth I. It was subsequently used as a Collect at Evening Prayer in the 1662 *Book of Common Prayer*, and in a modernised form in the *Alternative Service Book 1980*.

Against temptation

O my Saviour,
let me not fall by little and little,
or think myself able to bear
the indulgence of any known sin
because it seems so insignificant.
Keep me from sinful beginnings,
lest they lead me on
to sorrowful endings.

Charles Haddon Spurgeon 1834–92

CHARLES HADDON SPURGEON was an eminent Baptist
Minister, famed as a preacher of considerable gifts and
power.

For forgiveness

God of mercy and forgiveness,
For the times when our love of indulgence
   and ease have weakened our hold on spiritual
      things;
      pardon us.

For when we have not held our bodies in
      subjection,
   and have forgotten that they were meant
   to be temples of your Holy Spirit;
      pardon us.

For the times we have failed those who have
      trusted us,
   and have been concerned with ourselves
   when they needed our concern:
      pardon us.

For the times when we have failed in courage,
   when we have failed to take a stand for
      righteousness,
   when we have come to terms with evil in our
      own lives;
      pardon us.

And make us new,
in Jesus Christ our Lord.   Amen.

Kenneth Slack 1917–1986

KENNETH SLACK, writer and ecumenist, was a minister in
the United Reformed Church and the Director of Christian
Aid.

For strength

O Heavenly Father,
the Father of all wisdom,
    understanding, and true strength,
I beseech thee, look mercifully upon me,
and send thy Holy Spirit into my breast;
that when I must join to fight in the field
for the glory of thy holy name,
then I, being strengthened with the defence
    of thy right hand,
may manfully stand in the confession
    of thy faith and thy truth,
and continue in the same
unto the end of my life,
through our Lord Jesus Christ.

Nicholas Ridley ?1500–1555

NICHOLAS RIDLEY, successively Bishop of Rochester and
London, was executed by burning in the reign of Mary
Tudor.

For courage

O merciful God,
be thou now unto me a strong tower of defence,
    I humbly entreat thee.
Give me grace to await thy leisure,
and patiently to bear what thou doest unto me;
nothing doubting or mistrusting
    thy goodness towards me;
for thou knowest what is good for me
    better than I do.
Therefore do with me in all things
    what thou wilt;
only arm me, I beseech thee, with thine armour,
    that I may stand fast;
above all things, taking to me
    the shield of faith;
praying always that I may refer myself
    wholly to thy will,
    abiding thy pleasure,
and comforting myself in those troubles
    which it shall please thee to send me,
seeing such troubles are profitable for me;
and I am assuredly persuaded
that all thou doest cannot but be well;
and unto thee be all honour and glory.   Amen.

Lady Jane Dudley 1537–54

LADY JANE DUDLEY, commonly known as Lady Jane
Grey and briefly Queen of England, was condemned to the
Tower of London in 1553, where this prayer was written;
she was executed in February 1554, aged seventeen.

In time of doubt

As I was born naked
I was with sin bespaked,
At which when I awaked
My Soul and Spirit shaked.

A sin has me infected,
I am thereof detected;
Mercy I have neglected,
I fear I am rejected.

The Word I have misused,
Good Council too refused,
Thus I my Self abused.
How can I be excused?

Mercies Gate is locked,
Yea, up that way is blocked,
Yea some that there have knocked,
God at their cryes hath mocked.

Thus I have sin committed
And so my self out-witted,
Yea, and my Soul unfitted
To be to Heaven admitted.

O Lord! do not disdain me,
But kindly entertain me;
Yea in thy Faith maintain me,
And let thy Love contain me.

John Bunyan 1628–88

JOHN BUNYAN, famous as a writer and preacher, whose *The Pilgrim's Progress from this World to That which Is to Come* was written in the 1670s, partly in prison. This poem, 'The Awakened Child's Lament' of 1686, shows how, in spite of years of imprisonment, he continued to express his own religious views.

Weakness of faith

While faith is with me, I am blest;
It turns my darkest night to day;
But, while I clasp it to my breast,
I often feel it slide away.

What shall I do if all my love,
My hopes, my toil, are cast away?
And if there be no God above
To hear and bless me when I pray?

Oh, help me, God! For thou alone
Canst my distracted soul relieve.
Forsake it not: it is thine own,
Though weak, yet longing to believe.

Anne Brontë 1820–49

ANNE BRONTË, one of the famous Brontë sisters of
Haworth Parsonage. She wrote a book of poems with her
sisters Charlotte and Emily, and two novels, *Agnes Grey* and
The Tenant of Wildfell Hall.

In Bewilderment

O Lord our Redeemer,
we approach you for all who are let and hindered
    in their approach to you.
O living light, we pray to you
for all poor souls who once had light,
but now are vexed and dim.
There are those for whom the former things
    are passed away,
but all things are not yet made new.
They wander in pathless ways, far from rest,
and from the help of man.
Keep their faces still to the morning.
Keep their feet still in the living way.
Prepare within them the revelation of your Son.
Give them his gospel for a creating light;
so that a new world may arise from their void,
and in his grace they may become free indeed;
Through Jesus Christ our Lord.

Peter Taylor Forsyth 1848–1921

PETER TAYLOR FORSYTH was a Congregational minister,
and a theologian and writer of distinction.

For spiritual comfort

Comfort, we ask you, most gracious God,
all who are cast down and faint of heart
amidst the sorrows and difficulties of the world:
and grant that, by the quickening power
   of the Holy Spirit,
they may be lifted up to you
   with hope and courage,
and enabled to go upon their way
rejoicing in your love;
through Jesus Christ our Lord.

Richard Meaux Benson 1824–1915

RICHARD MEAUX BENSON was the Founder of the
Society of Mission Priests of St John the Evangelist.

For divine consolation

Let me never forget, O my God,
that seasons of consolation are refreshments here,
and nothing more;
not our abiding state.
They will not remain with us,
except in heaven.
Here they are only intended to prepare us
for doing and suffering.
I pray Thee, O my God,
to give them to me from time to time.
Shed over me the sweetness of Thy Presence,
lest I faint by the way;
lest I find religious service wearisome,
through my exceeding infirmity,
and give over prayer and meditation;
lest I go about my daily work in a dry spirit,
or am tempted to take pleasure in it
for its own sake, and not for Thee.
Give me Thy Divine consolations
from time to time;
but let me not rest in them.
Let me use them
for the purpose for which Thou givest them.
Let me not think it grievous,
let me not be downcast, if they go.
Let them carry me forward
to the thought and the desire of heaven.

John Henry Newman 1801–90

JOHN HENRY NEWMAN was a Fellow of Oriel College and a
leading Tractarian until he became a Roman Catholic in 1845. He
was made a Cardinal in 1879.

Hope

May the Lord be my friend,
Who once on earth endured on the gallows-tree
Suffered here for the sins of men.
He has redeemed us, he has given us life
And a home in Heaven. Hope was renewed
With bliss and blessing for those who had been
   through burning.
The Son was successful in that expedition,
Mighty in victory, when with a mass,
A great crowd of souls, came to God's kingdom
The Almighty Ruler, to joy among the angels
And all the saints, who in heaven already
Lived in glory, then the Lord,
Almighty God, came home to his own land.

Anon. Anglo-Saxon

This prayer comes from the conclusion of *The Dream of the
Rood*, an Anglo-Saxon poem by an anonymous writer,
telling of a vision of the Cross.

For health

God our Father,
you are the source of all health and healing,
all strength and peace.
Teach us to know you more truly
and to trust you more firmly.
Take from us all that hinders your healing power,
all anxieties and fears;
and help us in our weakness to rest in your love
and enter into the stillness of your presence;
Through Jesus Christ our Lord.

Donald Coggan 1909–

DONALD COGGAN, Archbishop of Canterbury from 1974
to 1980, has used this particular prayer a good deal,
especially during a teaching mission at the Christian
hospital complex at Vellore, South India.

Thanksgiving for healing

Almighty God, who hast restored light to my eye
and enabled me to pursue again
the studies which thou hast set before me:
Teach me, by the diminution of my sight,
to remember that whatever I possess is thy gift,
and by its recovery, to hope for thy mercy;
and, O Lord, take not thy Holy Spirit from me,
but grant that I may use thy bounties
according to thy will,
through Jesus Christ our Lord.

Samuel Johnson 1709–84

SAMUEL JOHNSON, famous eighteenth-century man of
letters and lexicographer, included among his considerable
literary output many prayers. This prayer was written on
15th February 1756, on the recovery of sight in one of his
eyes.

For healing for another

O most mighty God and merciful Father,
we most humbly beseech thee,
if it be thy good pleasure,
to continue to us that singular benefit
which thou hast given us
in the friendship of thy servant,
our dear brother,
who now lieth on the bed of sickness.
Let him abide with us yet awhile
for the furtherance of our faith;
yet awhile spare him,
that he may live to thy honour and our comfort.
Thou hast made him a great help
and furtherance of the best things among us.
O Lord, we beseech thee,
restore us our dear brother,
by restoring him to health.

Nicholas Ferrar 1592–1637

NICHOLAS FERRAR retired from Membership of the
House of Commons in 1625, to found a Community of lay
people at Little Gidding in Huntingdonshire, for prayer and
charitable works. The intention of this prayer was to ask for
healing in the grave illness of the priest and poet George
Herbert.

For the dying

O Lord Jesus Christ,
who in thy last agony
didst commend thy spirit into the hands
    of thy heavenly Father:
Have mercy upon all sick and dying persons:
may death be unto them the gate
    of everlasting life;
and give them the assurance of thy presence
even in the dark valley;
for thy name's sake
who art the resurrection and the life,
and to whom be glory for ever and ever.

Sarum Primer

The Sarum rite was in use in the middle ages (see note on
p. 35).

Fear of death

Wilt thou forgive that sin where I
      begun,
Which was my sin, though it were
      done before?
Wilt thou forgive that sin, through which I run
  And do run still, though still I do deplore?
   When thou hast done, thou hast not done;
     For I have more.

Wilt thou forgive that sin which I have won
  Others to sin, and made my sins their door?
Wilt thou forgive that sin which I did shun
  A year or two, but wallow'd in a score?
    When thou hast done, thou hast not done;
     For I have more.

I have a sin of fear, that when I've spun
  My last thread, I shall perish on the shore;
But swear by thyself, that at my death thy Son
  Shall shine, as He shines now and heretofore:
    And having done that, thou hast done;
     I fear no more.

John Donne 1573–1631

JOHN DONNE, poet and Dean of St Paul's from 1621 to
1631.

In face of death

Lord, I am coming as fast as I can.
I know I must pass through the shadow of death,
before I can come to see thee.
But it is but a mere shadow of death,
a little darkness upon nature;
but thou by thy merits and passion
Hast broke through the jaws of death.
So, Lord, receive my soul, and have mercy upon
    me;
and bless this kingdom with peace and plenty,
and with brotherly love and charity,
that there may not be this effusion of blood
    amongst them.
For Jesus Christ his sake, if it be thy will.

Lord, receive my soul.

William Laud 1573–1645

WILLIAM LAUD became Archbishop of Canterbury in
1633. Impeached by the Long Parliament, he was sent to the
Tower of London in 1641 and executed in 1645. This was his
prayer on the scaffold.

For a dying friend

Almighty and most merciful Father,
whose loving kindness is over all thy works;
Behold, visit and relieve
this thy servant who is grieved with sickness.
Grant that the sense of her weakness
may add strength to her faith,
and seriousness to her repentance.
And grant that, by the help of thy Holy Spirit,
after the pains and labours of this short life,
we may all obtain everlasting happiness,
through Jesus Christ our Lord:
for whose sake hear our prayers.   Amen.

Samuel Johnson 1709–84

SAMUEL JOHNSON, man of letters (see note on p. 96).
This prayer was written on Sunday, 18th October 1767,
when he paid a farewell visit to an old friend and prayed
with her.

On the death of a child

O God, you have dealt very mysteriously with us.
We have been passing through deep waters;
our feet were well-nigh gone.
But though you slay us, yet will we trust in you . . .
They are gone from us . . .
You have re-claimed the lent jewels.
Yet, O Lord, shall I not thank you now?
I will thank you not only for the children
     you have left to us,
but for those you have re-claimed.
I thank you for the blessing of the last ten years,
and for all the sweet memories of these lives . . .
I thank you for the full assurance that each has
     gone
to the arms of the Good Shepherd,
whom each loved according to the capacity of
     her years.
I thank you for the bright hopes of a happy
     reunion,
when we shall meet to part no more.
O Lord, for Jesus Christ's sake,
comfort our desolate hearts.
May we be a united family still in heart
through the communion of saints;
through Jesus Christ our Lord.

Archibald Campbell Tait 1811–82

ARCHIBALD CAMPELL TAIT became Dean of Carlisle in
1849; Bishop of London 1856 and Archbishop of Canterbury
1868. Between 11th March and 8th April 1856 at Carlisle,
Archibald Tait and his wife lost five of their six daughters of
scarlet fever; there remained a boy of six and a child in arms.

On the death of a dear one

O God, to me who am left to mourn his departure,
grant that I may not sorrow as one without hope
for my beloved who sleeps in you;
but, as always remembering his courage,
and the love that united us on earth,
I may begin again with new courage
    to serve you more fervently
who are the only source of true love
    and true fortitude;
that when I have passed a few more days
    in this valley of tears
    and this shadow of death,
supported by your rod and staff,
I may see him face to face,
in those pastures
and beside those waters of comfort
where I believe he already walks with you.
O Shepherd of the sheep,
have pity on this darkened soul of mine.

Edward White Benson 1829–96

EDWARD WHITE BENSON was Archbishop of Canterbury
from 1883 to 1896. This prayer was written on the death of
his son Martin as a schoolboy, in 1877.

The faithful departed

O Lord, we praise your holy name
for all your servants departed from us
in your faith and fear;
And we humbly beseech you to bless
us that remain on earth,
that, being protected from all evil,
ghostly and bodily,
we may ever serve and please you
with quiet minds and thankful hearts,
and together with those that are gone before
may have our refreshment in Paradise
and our portion in the Resurrection of the just;
through Jesus Christ our Lord.

Frederick Temple 1821–1902

FREDERICK TEMPLE was Archbishop of Canterbury from
1897 to 1902.

Thankfulness

Almighty God, Lord of Heaven and earth,
in whom we live and move and have our being;
who doest good unto all men,
making thy sun to rise on the evil and on the good,
and sending rain on the just and on the unjust;
Favourably behold us thy servants
who call upon thy name,
and send us thy blessing from heaven,
in giving us fruitful seasons,
and filling our hearts with food and gladness;
that both our hearts and mouths may be
    continually
filled with thy praise,
giving thanks to thee in thy holy Church,
through Jesus Christ our Lord.

John Cosin 1594–1672

JOHN COSIN was a composer of many prayers. His
Collection of Private Devotions was published in 1627, and he
contributed to the *Book of Common Prayer* of 1662. He became
Bishop of Durham in 1660.

Grace after dinner

The God of peace and love
vouchsafe always to dwell with us.
And thou, Lord, have mercy upon us.
Glory, honour and praise be to thee,
O God, who hast fed us from our tender age
and giveth sustenance to every living thing.
Replenish our hearts with love and gladness;
that we, always having sufficient,
may be rich and plentiful in all good works;
through our Lord Jesu Christ.   Amen.

The *Primer* of 1545

From the third Primer of the reign of Henry VIII, named
'King Henry's Primer'.

Grace before supper

O Lord Jesu Christ,
without whom nothing is sweet nor savoury,
we beseech thee to bless us and our supper,
and with thy blessed presence to cheer our hearts,
that in all our meats and drinks,
we may taste and savour of thee,
to thy honour and glory.

The *Primer* of 1545

Gratefulness

Thou that hast given so much to me,
Give one thing more, a grateful heart.
See how thy beggar work on thee
           By art.

He makes thy gifts occasion more.
And says, If he in this be crossed.
All thou hast given him heretofore
           Is lost.

But thou didst reckon, when at first
Thy word our hearts and hands did crave,
What it would come to at the worst
           To save.

Perpetual knockings at thy door,
Tears sullying thy transparent rooms,
Gift upon gift, much would have more,
           And comes.

This not withstanding, thou wentst on,
And didst allow us all our noise:
Nay thou hast made a sigh and groan
           Thy joys.

Not that thou hast not still above
Much better tunes, than groans can make;
But that these country-airs thy love
           Did take.

Wherefore I cry and cry again;
And in no quiet canst thou be,
Till I a thankful heart obtain
                              Of thee:

Not thankful, when it pleaseth me;
As if thy blessings had spare days:
But such a heart, whose pulse may be
                              Thy praise.

George Herbert 1593–1633

GEORGE HERBERT, priest and poet, was Rector of
Bemerton in Wiltshire from 1630 to 1633. His poetry was
mainly of a devotional character.

Thanksgiving

I thank thee, O Lord, my Lord,
> for my being,
>> my life,
>> my gift of reason;
> for my nurture,
>> my preservation,
>> my guidance;
> for my education,
>> my civil rights,
>> my religious privileges;
> for thy gifts of grace,
>>> of nature,
>>> of this world;
> for my redemption,
>> my regeneration,
>> my instruction in the Christian Faith;
> for my calling,
>> my recalling,
>> my manifold renewed recalling;

> for thy forbearance and long-suffering,
>> thy prolonged forbearance, many a time,
>>> and many a year;
> for all the benefits I have received,
>> and all the undertakings wherein I have
>>> prospered;
> for any good I may have done;
> for the use of the blessings of this life;
> for thy promise,
>> and my hope of the enjoyment of good
>>> things to come;

for good and honest parents,
  gentle teachers,
  benefactors ever to be remembered,
  congenial companions,
  intelligent hearers,
  sincere friends,
  faithful servants;
for all who have profited me by their
                                    writings,
                                    sermons,
                                    conversations,
                                    prayers,
                                    examples,
                                    reproofs,
                                    injuries;
for all these and also for all other mercies,
known and unknown,
open and secret,
remembered by me, or now forgotten,
kindnesses received by me willingly, or
    even against my will,
I praise thee, I bless thee, I thank thee,
and will praise and bless and thank thee,
    all the days of my life.

Lancelot Andrewes 1555–1626

LANCELOT ANDREWES, author of *Preces Privatae* (see note on p. 79).